I0821921

GROSS JOBS Working with GARBAGE

An Augmented Reading Experience

by Nikki Bruno

CAPSTONE PRESS
a capstone imprint

Blazers Books are published by Capstone Press,
1710 Roe Crest Drive, North Mankato, Minnesota 56003
www.mycapstone.com

Library of Congress Cataloging-in-Publication data is available on the Library of Congress website.
ISBN: 978-1-5435-5487-8 (hardcover)
ISBN: 978-1-5435-5896-8 (paperback)
ISBN: 978-1-5435-5493-9 (eBook PDF)
Summary: A close look at gross jobs in the field of waste removal.

Editorial Credits
Hank Musolf, editor; Bobbie Nuytten, designer; Heather Mauldin, media researcher; Katy LaVigne, production specialist

Photo Credits
Alamy: Paulo Oliveira, 22 (inset); ASSOCIATED PRESS: Ingo Wagner/picture-alliance/dpa, 19, Lake Charles American Press, Brad Puckett, 8-9; Getty Images: Bryan Chan/Los Angeles Times, 10-11, Gordon Chibroski/Portland Press Herald, 26-27, Justin Sullivan, 20-21, KATHERINE HADDON/AFP, 8 (inset), MOHAMMED ABED/AFP, 24-25, TED ALJIBE/AFP, 16-17, Tom Pennington/Stringer, 12-13; iStockphoto: burdem, 22-23, PeopleImages, 6-7, Ralph125, 14 (inset), vm, cover, 1, WALTER ZERLA, 14-15; Shutterstock: David Litman, 18, ducu59us, 4-5, Lorenzo Sala, 20 (inset), MikeDotta, 6 (inset), project1photography, 29
Design Elements
Shutterstock: Alhovik, kasha_malasha, Katsiaryna Chumakova, Yellow Stocking

Printed and bound in the United States of America.
PA48

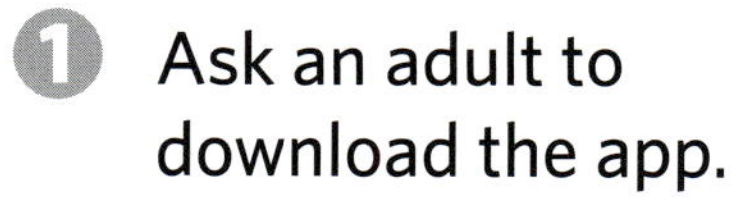

2 Scan any page with the star.

3 Enjoy your cool stuff!

OR

Use this password at capstone4D.com

garbage.54879

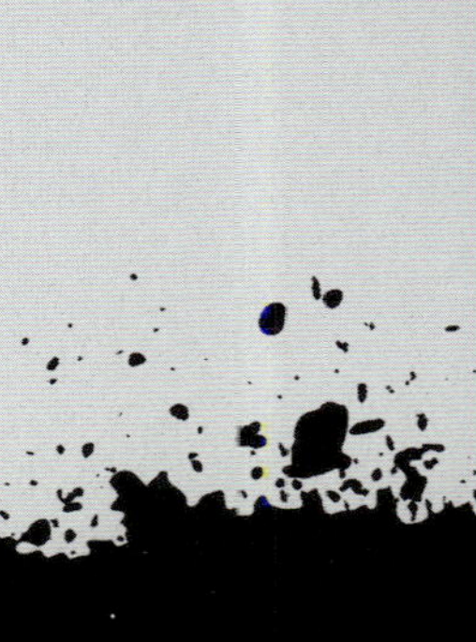

TABLE OF CONTENTS

Working with Waste 4
Garbage Collector 6
Roadkill Remover 8
Crime Scene Cleaner 10
School Custodian 12
Landfill Worker 14
Methane Gas Operator 16
Vomit Cleaner 18
Compost Center Worker 20
Ocean Trash Collector 22
Medical Waste Cooker 24
Sludge Cleaner 26
Hats Off to Our Workers! 28

Glossary 30
Read More 31
Internet Sites 31
Index 32

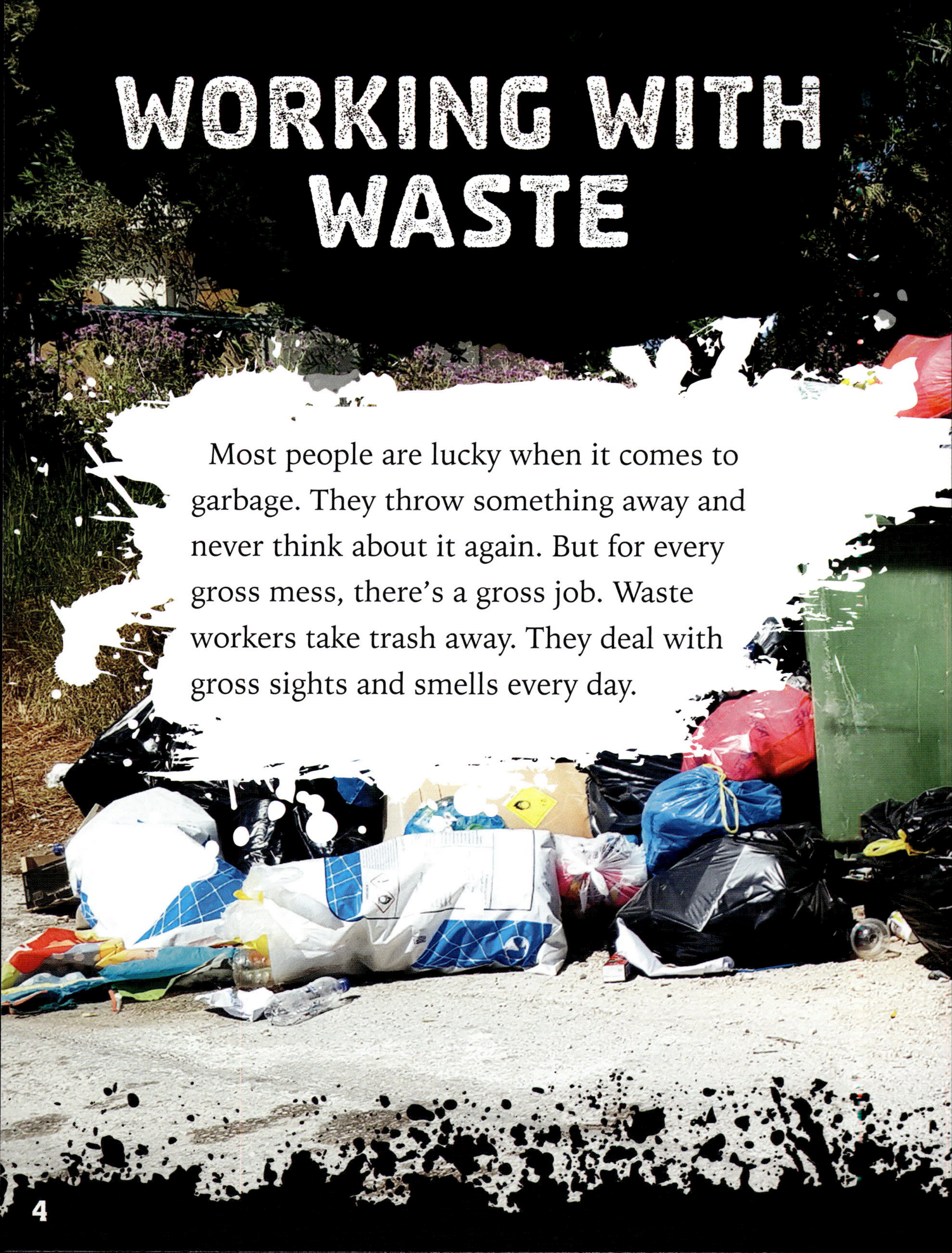

WORKING WITH WASTE

Most people are lucky when it comes to garbage. They throw something away and never think about it again. But for every gross mess, there's a gross job. Waste workers take trash away. They deal with gross sights and smells every day.

GARBAGE COLLECTOR

Garbage collectors are at work before sunrise. They load their trucks with rotten food, snotty tissues, dog poop, and other trash. The sour smell of garbage follows them until they unload it at the dump.

DID YOU KNOW?

In a year, the United States creates about 250 million tons (227 million metric tons) of garbage.

ROADKILL REMOVER

Roadkill removers find and get rid of animals killed by cars and trucks. These workers handle dead deer, squirrels, raccoons, and more. They also deal with flies and **maggots**. These critters love to hang out on or near roadkill.

DID YOU KNOW?

Sometimes workers don't get rid of the bodies right away. They store the animal bodies in freezers.

roadkill—an animal that has been killed and partly flattened by a vehicle

maggot—the larva of certain flies

CRIME SCENE CLEANER

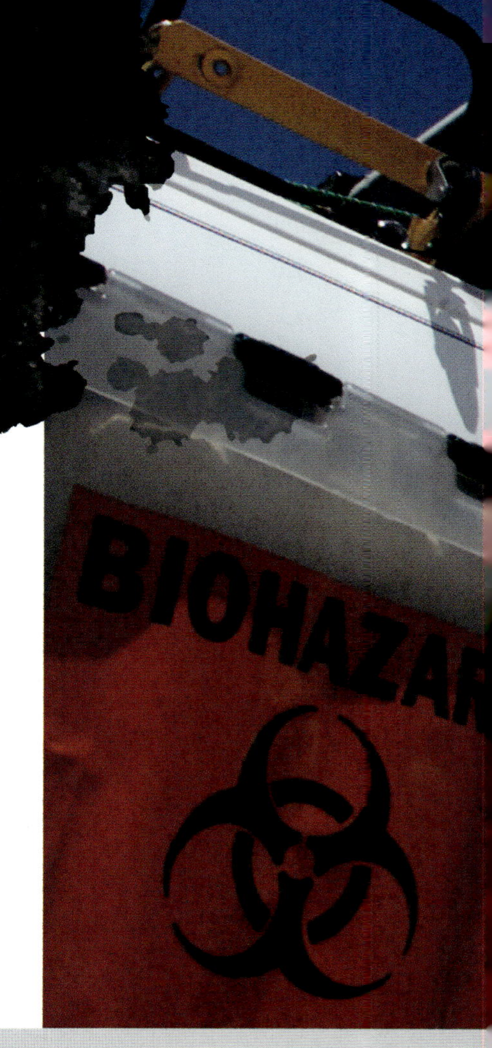

Crime scene cleaners help out after a violent crime or an accident. They handle human blood and other bodily fluids. Special suits and masks keep cleaners safe from disease and horrible smells.

DID YOU KNOW?

Some crime scene cleaners are hired to do other jobs. They clean up houses that have too much garbage in them.

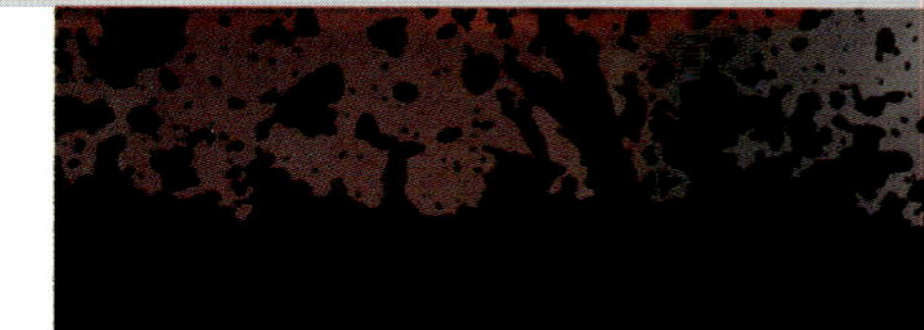

SCHOOL CUSTODIAN

School custodians clean up students' everyday messes. Some kids stick chewed gum under desks. Others might get sick and throw up. School bathrooms can quickly get dirty and stinky. Thanks to custodians, these messes don't last long.

DID YOU KNOW?

School custodians do a lot more than cleaning. They control heating and cooling systems. They also make sure machines in the school run well.

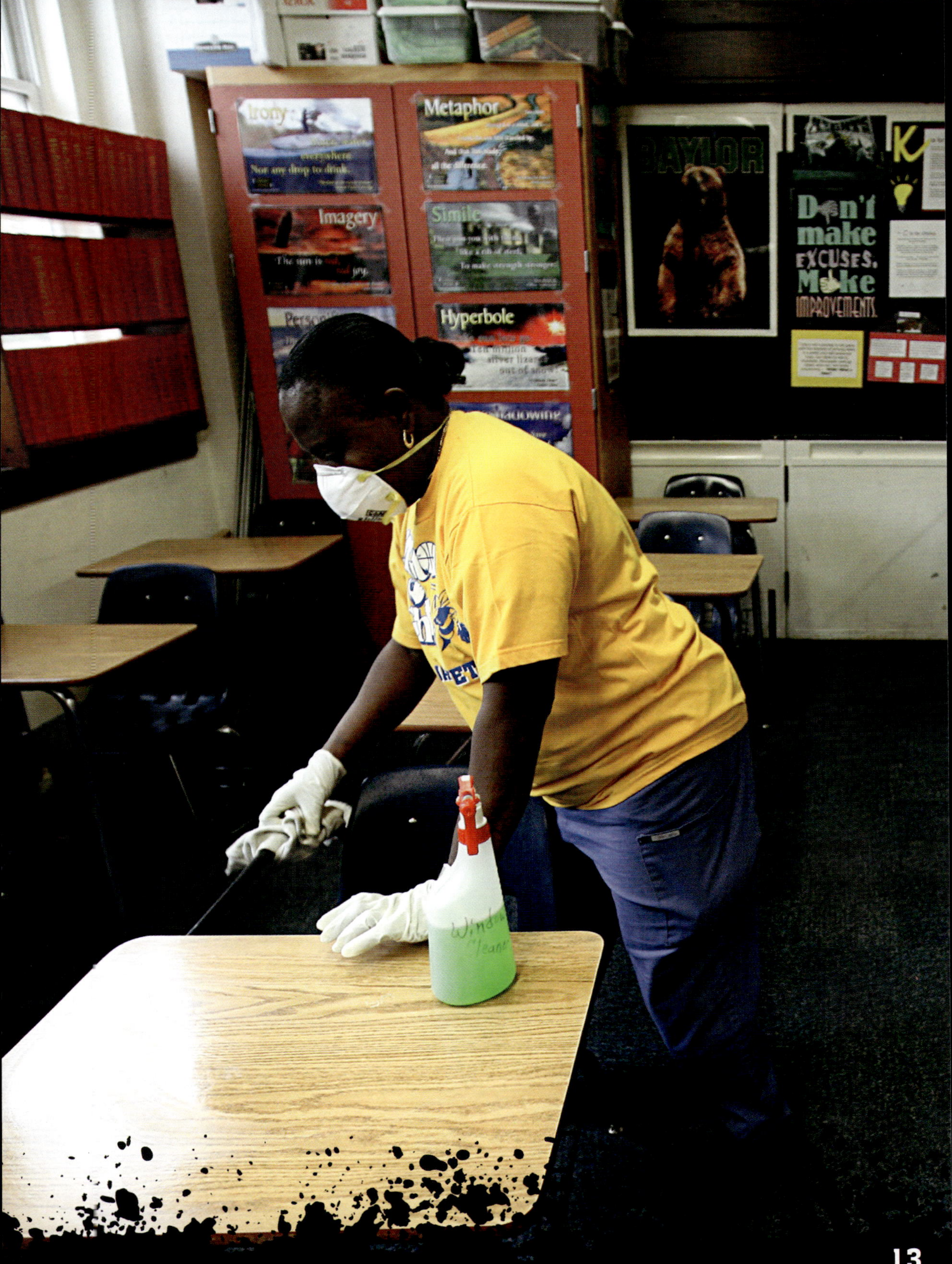
Irony
Nor any drop to drink.
Metaphor
Imagery
Simile
Hyperbole
BAYLOR
Don't make EXCUSES. Make IMPROVEMENTS.

LANDFILL WORKER

A **landfill** is a huge outdoor area filled with trash. Tons of garbage ends up there, from dirty diapers to rotten food. Landfill workers spend their days in these gross places. They sort waste and put it in the right places.

GROSS-O-METER

DID YOU KNOW?

There are around 2,000 active landfills in the United States. Another 10,000 old landfills in the U.S. are closed.

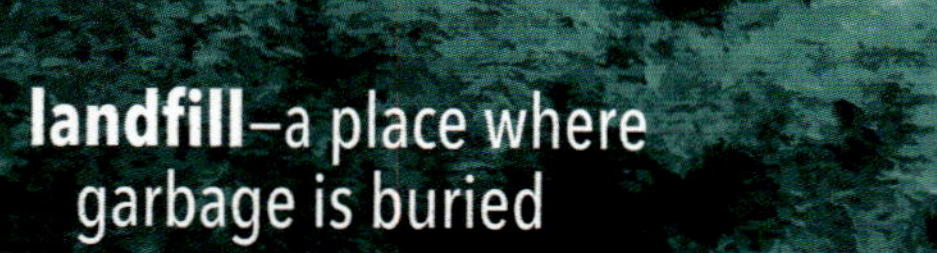

landfill—a place where garbage is buried

METHANE GAS OPERATOR

Trash releases stinky gases. **Methane** can be used to make electricity. This gas is collected in holes drilled in landfills. A gas operator makes sure the gas moves from the holes into pipes. The gas goes to a power plant that turns it into electricity.

TRADE GAS FOR ENERGY

Methane is a greenhouse gas. It traps heat near Earth and makes the air hotter. The more methane we collect, the better off Earth will be.

methane—a colorless, flammable gas produced by decay of plant and animal matter

I-9

VOMIT CLEANER

Theme parks are supposed to be fun. But wild rides make some people throw up. Vomit cleaners use **absorbent** powder and special tools. They collect the goo and remove the smell.

DID YOU KNOW?

A company offers a wild plane ride called the Vomit Comet. It makes such fast loops that riders will feel like they're in space. Many people throw up on it!

absorbent—the ability to soak up liquid

COMPOST CENTER WORKER

Compost trucks drop off maggot-covered meat, stinky eggshells, used tissues, and human hair. Workers stir the garbage to break it down. In time it can be added to dirt.

DID YOU KNOW?

Wild animals such as mice, rats, or birds may sneak into compost bins and get trapped. Compost workers find their dead bodies there.

compost—a mixture of rotted leaves, vegetables, manure, and other items that are added to soil to make it richer

Recology
Sunset Scavenger
BLES

OCEAN TRASH COLLECTOR

Earth's oceans have huge areas of floating trash. The biggest patch is about twice as big as Texas. Companies hire workers to do ocean cleanups. Collectors lower a machine into the ocean that picks up trash. The workers sort through the garbage.

KILLER TRASH!

Trash kills thousands of ocean animals every year. For example, turtles eat balloon pieces and stop breathing. Whales may eat too much plastic and die.

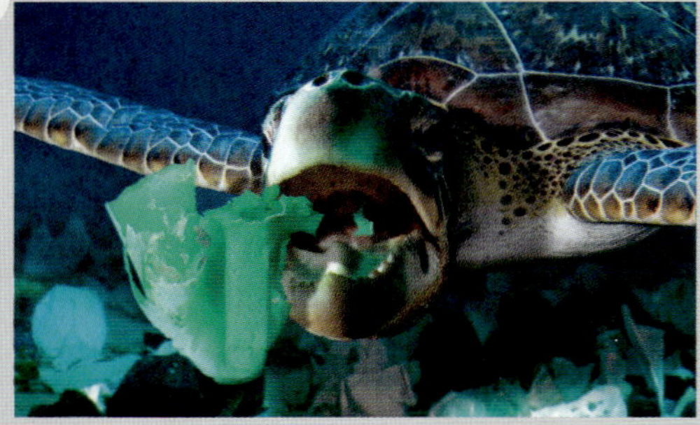

MEDICAL WASTE COOKER

Some of the grossest waste comes from the human body. Medical waste cookers work in hospitals. They deal with blood, poop, urine, snot, **pus**, and vomit. This waste can spread deadly diseases. Waste cookers burn it in **incinerators**.

DID YOU KNOW?

Workers steam medical waste in a container called an autoclave. The steam must be hotter than 250° degrees Fahrenheit (121° degrees Celsius) to kill germs.

pus—a yellowish-white fluid found in sores and infections

incinerator—a furnace for burning garbage and other waste materials

SLUDGE CLEANER

Sludge is a mixture of oil, grease, dirt, and water. It forms inside engines and at sewage plants. Sludge cleaners wear waterproof suits. They vacuum hot, smelly fluid out of collection tanks.

DID YOU KNOW?

Sludge cleaners sometimes get sludge on their skin. Sometimes they clean it off with soap and sugar.

HATS OFF TO OUR WORKERS!

Without waste workers, the world would be a much dirtier and more dangerous place. These workers deal with gross germs and goopy messes to keep the world cleaner. Their work keeps everyone healthier and safer.

GLOSSARY

absorbent (ub-SOR-bent)–the ability to soak up liquid

compost (KAHM-post)–a mixture of rotted leaves, vegetables, manure, and other items that are added to soil to make it richer

incinerator (in-SIN-er-ay-ter)–a furnace for burning garbage and other waste materials

landfill (LAND-fil)–a place where garbage is buried

maggot (MAG-it)–the larva of certain flies

methane (METH-ayne)–a colorless, flammable gas produced by decay of plant and animal matter

pus (PUHSS)–a yellowish-white fluid found in sores and infections

roadkill (ROHD-kil)–an animal that has been killed and partly flattened by a vehicle, such as a car or truck

READ MORE

Duhaime, Darla. *Gross Jobs*. Gross Me Out! Vero Beach, Fla.: Rourke Educational Media, 2016.

Miller, Mirella S. *Compost Center Operator*. Gross Jobs. Mankato, Minn.: Childs World, 2015.

Vonne, Mira. *Gross Facts About the Middle Ages*. Gross History. North Mankato, Minn.: Capstone Press, 2017.

INTERNET SITES

Use FactHound to find Internet sites related to this book.

Visit *www.facthound.com*

Just type in 9781543554878 and go.

INDEX

absorbent powder, 18

bathrooms, 12
blood, 10, 24
body fluids, 10, 24

chewing gum, 12
compost, 20

dead animals, 8, 20, 22
dirty diapers, 14
diseases, 10, 24
dumps (or landfills), 6, 14, 16

electricity, 16

hair, 20

incinerators, 24

maggots, 8, 20
methane, 16

ocean cleanups, 22

poop, 6, 24

rotten food, 6, 14, 20

safety equipment, 10, 18, 22, 24, 26
sludge, 26
snot, 6, 24

theme parks, 18

vomit, 12, 18, 24